History in Living Memory

Entertainment
Through the Years

How having fun
has changed in
living memory

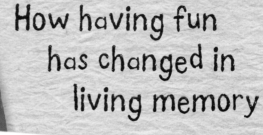

Clare Lewis

Raintree is an imprint of Capstone Global Library Limited, a company incorporated in England and Wales having its registered office at 7 Pilgrim Street, London, EC4V 6LB – Registered company number: 6695582

www.raintree.co.uk
myorders@raintree.co.uk

Edited by Clare Lewis and Holly Beaumont
Designed by Philippa Jenkins
Picture research by Tracy Cummins
Production by Victoria Fitzgerald
Originated by Capstone Global Library Ltd
Printed and bound in China by Leo Paper Group

ISBN 978 1 406 29012 7 (hardback)
18 17 16 15 14
10 9 8 7 6 5 4 3 2 1

ISBN 978 1 406 29017 2 (paperback)
19 18 17 16 15
10 9 8 7 6 5 4 3 2 1

British Library Cataloguing in Publication Data
A full catalogue record for this book is available from the British Library.

Acknowledgements
We would like to thank the following for permission to reproduce photographs: Capstone Press: Philippa Jenkins, 1 Bottom Right, 1 Top Left; Corbis: ©D&P Valenti/ClassicStock, 17; Corel: 4; Flickr: John Atherton, Cover Top; Getty Images: David Hanover, 19, Gamma-Keystone, 12, Imagno, 15, L. Willinger/FPG/Hulton Archive, 14, Richi Howell/Redferns, 9; Shutterstock: aopsan, 23 Top, AVAVA, Cover Bottom, Dan Kosmayer, 23 Middle, Diego Cervo, 20, Flas100, Design Element, Panom Pensawang, 22 Top Right, racorn, 22 Bottom, Samuel Borges Photography, 21, Studio DMM Photography, Designs & Art, Design Element, Vector Department, 23 Bottom, ZanyZeus, 22 Top Left; SuperStock: ClassicStock.com, 5, 8, 10, Cusp, 16, Marka, 6, Superstock, 7, Transtock, 11, 13; Thinkstock: Creatas, 18, Back Cover.

Every effort has been made to contact copyright holders of material reproduced in this book. Any omissions will be rectified in subsequent printings if notice is given to the publisher. All the internet addresses (URLs) given in this book were valid at the time of going to press. However, due to the dynamic nature of the internet, some addresses may have changed, or sites may have changed or ceased to exist since publication. While the author and publisher regret any inconvenience this may cause readers, no responsibility for any such changes can be accepted by either the author or the publisher.

Some words are shown in bold, **like this**. You can find them in the glossary on page 23.

Contents

What is history in living memory?

Some history happened a very long time ago. Nobody alive now lived through it.

Some history did not happen so long ago.
Our parents, grandparents and adult
friends can tell us how life used to be.
We call this history in living memory.

How has entertainment changed in living memory?

The way people have fun has changed a lot since your grandparents were young. In the 1950s, there were no mobile phones or computers.

Children listened to programmes on the radio. They watched black-and-white films at the cinema.

How did people listen to music in the 1950s?

People listened to music on the radio or on **record** players. In the 1950s, a new type of music called rock and roll became popular.

People loved to dance to rock and roll music. Teenagers gathered around record shops to hear the new songs.

How did people have fun in the 1960s?

In the 1960s, more people had televisions. Television programmes were now in colour.

Like today, going to the cinema was a fun treat. *Mary Poppins* was a popular film in the 1960s.

How did your parents and grandparents play?

In the olden days, there were fewer cars. Children played outside more than they do now.

Children climbed trees, skipped and played football. Children still do these things today.

How did children have fun in the 1970s?

In the 1970s, Barbie dolls were a popular toy. Children also played board games, **marbles** and hide-and-seek.

Just like today, people enjoyed trips out with their family to museums. Museums weren't as hands-on as they are today.

What changes happened in the 1980s?

In the 1980s, **cassettes** began to be used to store and play music. Portable cassette players allowed people to listen to music while moving around outside.

Some people had computers at home for playing games. It could take 30 minutes for a game to load in those days!

How did people have fun in the 1990s?

In the 1990s, most people listened to music on CDs. Games consoles also became very popular and easier to use.

The internet became popular in the late 1990s. This made it easier for people from all over the world to talk together, play games together and share ideas.

How do you have fun today?

Some things haven't changed in living memory. We still like to read books and play outside with our friends.

Some things have changed a lot.
How do you play games and listen
to music now?

Picture quiz

Which of these could be played in the 1970s?

marbles

tablet games

games console

How is this game different from many games you play today?

Picture glossary

cassette
small case with coiled tape inside. It was used for recording and playing music in the 1970s and 1980s.

marbles
coloured glass balls used for playing games

record
round flat piece of plastic. It was used for recording and playing music in the 1960s and 1970s.

Find out more

Books

In the Past: Toys, Dereen Taylor (Wayland, 2010)

Toys and Games (Ways into History), Sally Hewitt (Franklin Watts, 2012)

Websites

www.bbc.co.uk/scotland/education/as/sixties
Find out what Scotland was like in the 1960s.

www.bbc.co.uk/schoolradio/subjects/history/britainsince1930s
Listen to audio clips about life in the past.

Index